THE GILCHRIST GIRLS

A TRIP TO YAYA'S

THE GREAT MOUSE ADVENTURE

The Adventures of Amelia, Ella and Isla

Written by JD Conselyea

Watercolor illustrations by Nicole Pontier-Carrels

For all Girls & Boys

Dedicated to Amelia, Ella & Isla

.1

Amelia and Ella were sisters but they were not
at all a like!

Amelia was six, tall and slender, the oldest of the
girls. She had long blonde hair and blue eyes.

She loved dancing and art and playing the
violin like her mother.

Ella was three and a half, robust with fiery, curly
red hair and blue eyes and like a boy she loved
running and jumping and climbing. The one
thing they had in common was a love of
adventure!

.3

In the summer the girls liked to travel with Momma and Daddy! They liked to visit their YAYA. Every summer they would travel to Helena, Montana and stay with Momma's Mother, whom they called "YAYA." This was a name used by the Native Americans for the grandmother on the mother's side. The girls were not Native American but they had a deep and abiding respect for the traditions of the Native people!

The girls honored the native people's love of the Earth and all the creatures that inhabited the sky, land and water.

.5

YAYA lived in the forest outside of Helena, Montana. In the North Hills where YAYA lived there were herds of White Tail Deer and Elk.

Snowshoe Rabbits hopped lickety- split through the forest. Turning white in the winter, so they did not stand out against the back drop of snow that covered the forest floor from December through March.

A family of cotton tail rabbits lived under YAYA's shed. Wild Turkeys roamed the hillside. Many variety of birds, some big, some small, came to roost and have their young in the bird houses posted on the Ponderosa Pine trees.

Amelia's favorite was the little Rocky Mountain Bluebird.

Their color was the most beautiful blue she had ever seen.

7.

YAYA lived with three cats. A nineteen year old male Siamese, named Mozart, a thirteen year old Calico female named Chloe and a ten year old bob-tailed, female Manx named Ishibia Ocheshewa. This was a Crow Indian name for Bob Cat. YAYA called her Ishi. She had one dog. A black, eleven year old female; mixed breed, Setter/Labrador, named Cassie.

Cassie was very sweet but very excitable and loved it when Amelia and Ella came to visit. She got so excited that she jumped up and down, wagging her tail uncontrollably.

She was so happy but this did not make Amelia and Ella's Momma happy. Fortunately, Cassie only jumped up and down for a few minutes. Soon the girls were running and playing ball with her, which was why she jumped up and down in the first place! She just wanted their attention.

Cassie loved her beat up old tennis balls that YAYA kept in the garage for her to play with. The girls knew right where to find them. Soon the girls and Cassie were playing fetch on the grass, while Momma and YAYA un- packed the car and carried the suitcases in to the house.

When it was time to put grain out for all the animals, usually about 4:30 in the afternoon, YAYA would call the girls and they would go together to the shed where the grain was kept in the big blue bin.

 YAYA would scoop the grain out with an old coffee can into a bucket. When it was full, she and the girls would carry it down to the old wood pallet. The girls would take turns scooping out the grain into each section. Once they had filled the pallet, they would carry the bucket to each pan YAYA had placed under the trees in the forest.

.9

Sharing and taking turns they filled each pan,

until the bucket was empty.

After all the animals had been fed, including Cassie and the cats. Amelia, Ella, Momma and YAYA would have dinner in the Sun Room. Ella loved the Sun Room!

She had to remember NOT to pick the Geraniums which grew profusely in the bright yellow room, with the panoramic view of the mountains, lake and forest. Amelia was older so she knew better than to pick the flowers in the Sun Room! She had learned that the blooms would last longer if they were allowed to stay on the plant! She would then be able to enjoy their beauty for her entire trip to YAYA's.

.11

The girls, when asked where they wanted to eat always chose the sun room!

One day when Amelia and Ella were visiting YAYA, Momma asked if they could all go for a ride in YAYA's 1990 black, Jeep Wrangler. YAYA said yes. She and the girls went out to start the car but it would not start! The girls were disappointed but YAYA told them not to worry. She would charge the battery and they would be able to drive out to the lake.

Amelia and Ella watched as YAYA unhooked the hood latches on each side and lifted the hood. Amelia let out a little squeal when she saw the Mama Mouse leap from the soft, furry nest sitting on the car battery.

Ella pointed with her finger and said, "look YAYA a baby mouse!" YAYA and Amelia looked to where Ella was pointing. A tiny, little mouse, no bigger than Ella's finger, peeked out of a soft ball of brown fur and grass.

.13

YAYA said, "WELL! Now we know why the car would not start but Mama Mouse and her babies cannot live on my car battery. We will need to move their home to a safer location."

She asked Amelia to bring her the dust pan and broom. Amelia was a good listener and she always did what her YAYA asked her to do! She knew it was important to listen to her parents and her teachers.

Soon YAYA had the dust pan and broom in her hands and she was gently scraping the nest from off the battery into the dust pan, being very careful to keep it in tact. After all, Mama Mouse had gone to a great deal of work to build such a magnificent house for her babies. YAYA did not want to destroy her home!

YAYA was not sure where to relocate the nest where it would be safe from the wind and where a wandering cat, or a hungry Bull Snake, or even Cassie would not disturb it. Then she saw the wood pile stacked outside of the garage on the wood pallets and she knew instantly where to put the little mouse's house.

.15

"Amelila, Ella, come quickly," YAYA called, "I know where we can put the little nest! It will be safe and the Mama Mouse will be able to find it and her babies, if they are still inside." The girls came running to her side, Ella got there first because she was always the fastest runner. "Where, where can we put it YAYA?" Amelia asked. Before YAYA could reply, as always, Ella echoed her big sister's words. "Where can we put it YAYA?" YAYA walked over to the wood pile and pointed to the exposed boards that would provide shelter but also allowed access for YAYA to gently place the nest under the boards.

Once the nest was safely under the pallet boards and YAYA, Amelia and Ella were confident that the little nest was in a safe place; they went back into the garage where YAYA installed the cables on the battery.

While Amelia and Ella waited for the battery to charge they helped YAYA put water in the

bird bath and seed in the bird feeders. YAYA suggested they sit on the deck and have hot chocolate with whipping cream and watch the birds. The girls thought this was a splendid idea! Racing to the front deck, seating themselves on the Redwood steps, enjoying the warm sunshine they waited patiently. YAYA went into the house

.17

to make the hot chocolate. "Don't forget the whipping cream YAYA," Amelia called out. Ella echoed her sister's request. Soon Momma, Amelia and Ella were enjoying hot chocolate, heaped high with whipping cream, in their favorite angel mugs. YAYA sipped her tea, as they watched the little Chickadees splashing in the bird bath underneath the tall Pine trees.

Suddenly a flock of wild Turkeys appeared. They scurried between the trees looking for bird seed that had spilled out of the feeders on to the ground. Amelia and Ella watched quietly, with a curious intensity, as the big birds hunted and pecked for food. Disappearing out of view, just as quickly as they had appeared.

YAYA explained to the girls that all creatures both great and small must be cared for. "All peoples of the Earth are caretakers! If the planet and the creatures are to survive we must all do our part to help one another. All life is one and interconnected!" "But YAYA," Ella replied looking very perplexed. "I don't look like a Turkey! How can I be one with a Turkey?" YAYA responded, a warm smile on her face. "You don't have to look like something to be one with it. We are all made of the same elements! The same stuff as the stars! It is just arranged differently and each unique arrangement creates something different."

"Well," Amelia said after listening carefully.

"I am glad I am arranged a girl and not a star!"
"I am glad you and Ella are not stars in the sky
too. I love you both very much!" Momma said.

"I know you both will be good caretakers!" YAYA said it was time to go and see if the car would start so they could drive out to the lake. The girls asked if they could go with YAYA and Momma said they could. When they got to the garage YAYA unhooked the battery cables and closed the hood. She was not sure where the Mama Mouse went when it ran out of the nest. YAYA did not know if she was still in the engine compartment, or if she had leapt to the floor.

She was not sure what would happen when she started the car. YAYA asked the girls to stand away from the car while she started it and backed it out of the garage. The girls did as their YAYA asked and stood very still, like statutes! YAYA climbed into the car and turned the key. Soon a "chugga," "chugga" sound could be heard and within moments the engine roared and YAYA was able to back the car

.21

out of the garage. She stopped it beside the wood pile and turned the engine off. Once the engine was off Amelia came running to tell her that she had seen the Mama Mouse jump from the car and run under the wood pile.

Moments later Ella came running to tell YAYA that there was a baby mouse on the floor of the garage. Taking Ella's hand, YAYA and Amelia entered the garage. Ella took them both to where the baby mouse lay on the cement floor. YAYA scooped up the tiny, little mouse in the dust pan. Gently, she carried it out to the wood pile where the nest was and placed the little baby back in the nest.

They all had high hopes that Mama Mouse would find her home and her baby! Now that they were all safely under the wood pile.

The very next morning, Amelia asked her Momma and YAYA if she and Ella could go out and see if the Mama Mouse had found

her home and her little baby.

.23

Amelia's Momma said she and YAYA would go with the girls to check on the nest. When all four of them arrived at the wood pile where YAYA and the girls had safely placed the nest, to their astonishment not a trace of it could be seen!

"Momma! YAYA!" Ella called out passionately. "It's gone! The mouse's house is gone! Where could it be?" YAYA got down on her knees and looked under the wood pallet to see if she could see it. As it was no longer where she and the girls had placed it the day before. The girls were very worried, tears were running down Ella's face and Amelia held tightly to her mother's hand.

YAYA replied reassuringly. "Look all around the wood pile and see if the wind or perhaps an animal has disturbed it. If this has happened we will surely find some remnants of the little nest. This may give us a clue as to what happened.

Ella wiped her tears and Amelia let go of her Momma's hand. "Ella," Amelia called out, "you look on the side by the tree and I will look on the side by the garage." Ella responded to her big sister's request and dutifully ran around the wood pile and began looking for any sign of the nest but found nothing. Amelia hurried to the other side and looked carefully but she too found no sign of the mouse's house. Not any fur was to be seen anywhere! Amelia and Ella's Momma shook her head sadly as the girls returned to her side.

"Don't be sad girls," YAYA said, "I think I know what happened to the little nest and the baby mouse." The girls jumped up and down with excitement. "Tell us YAYA," Amelia responded. Of course, Ella echoed her big sister's words. "Yes, tell us YAYA, what happened to the nest and the baby mouse."

.25

"I believe the "Creator" guided Mama Mouse
to her baby and her home and she has moved
It farther under the wood pile so she and the
little mouse will be safer from the wind, the rain

and any large animal. If the wind or an animal had disturbed the nest you girls would have surely found some evidence of this and as Amelia found nothing." YAYA looked at Amelia, who shook her head from side to side. "And Ella found nothing," who also shook her head from side to side. "I believe we are quite safe in believing that it was Mama Mouse who found and moved her house!"

A Gilchrist Girls country adventure, with a very happy ending for Mama Mouse's tale!

The End